Comprehension Reader

Intermediate

⟨ℂ Harcourt School Publishers

www.harcourtschool.com

Printed in the United States of America

ISBN 10 0-15-368094-6

ISBN 13 978-0-15-368094-6

 2 3 4 5 6 7 8 9 10 197 16 15 14 13 12 11 10 09 08

CONTENTS

1: Anna's Apple Dolls   4

2: Auction Day   12

3: Race to the Sea   20

4: A Troublesome Nose   28

5: Raindrop in the Sun   36

6: Room to Share   44

7: An American Legend   52

8: Fire in the Forest   60

9: Desert Animals   68

10: Frontier Children   76

11: Bringing Back the Puffins   84

12: Sisters Forever   92

13: **Blizzard Season**   100

14: **Cindy "Science" Spots the Clues**   108

15: **Hello from Here**   116

16: **Click!**   124

17: **Joe DiMaggio: One of Baseball's Greatest**   132

18: **Gardens of the Sea: Coral Reefs**   140

19: **A Mountain Blows Its Top**   148

20: **A Place of New Beginnings**   156

21: **The Krakatoa Wave**   164

22: **The Little Brown Quail**   172

23: **A Clever Plan**   180

24: **Book of Days**   188

Anna's Apple Dolls

by Meish Goldish

illustrated by Tom Casmer

Setting: *A frontier cabin in the west.*

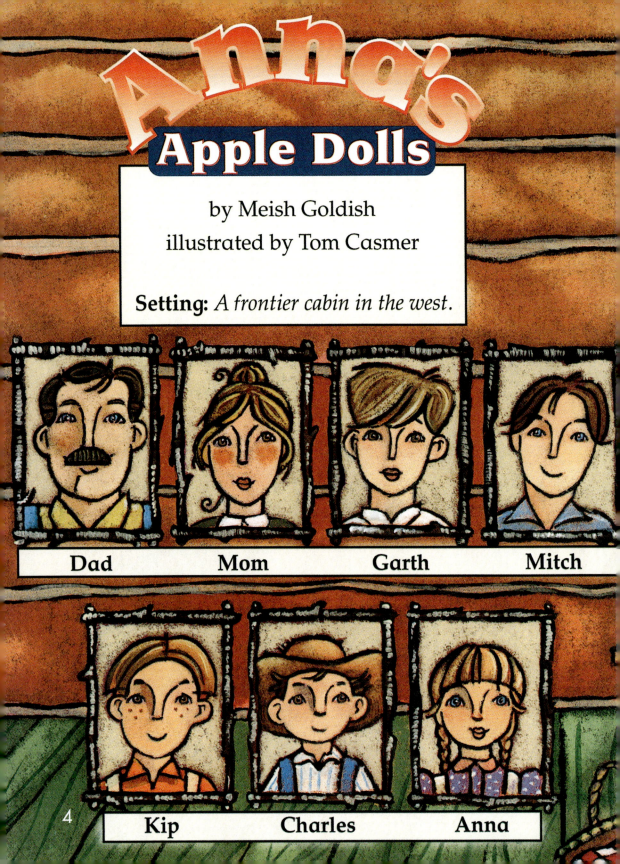

Dad Mom Garth Mitch

Kip Charles Anna

Anna: Mom?

Mom: What is it, Anna?

Anna: I did all my work. May I go outdoors now? May I play in the apple orchard?

Mom: Yes, you may, Anna. Take a basket and get some apples, too. Get a big batch for the family.

Anna: All right. I'll bring as many as I can.

(*Anna takes a basket and walks out.*)

Setting: *On the path to the orchard.*

Charles: Well, look who's here! It's little Anna!

Kip: Anna! Why are you outdoors? A wild animal may be nearby. It could catch you!

Mitch: Could you survive, Anna? Could you tame a wild animal?

Garth: All right, you three. Let Anna be. She is your sis, after all.

Anna: Yes, and I can work just as hard as you can!

Charles: Can you chop a tree?

Kip: Can you dig a ditch?

Mitch: Can you catch a fish?

Anna: No, but I can pick apples for our family. I'll pick a big batch of them! You just watch and see.

Garth: I'll go with you, Anna. We'll have fun picking apples.

(Anna and Garth walk away.)

8

Setting: *Outdoors at the orchard.*

Anna: These trees are so tall, Garth! Which apples will you pick? Watch what you are doing up there. Your feet may slip.

Garth: I'm OK, Anna. We can get lots of apples here!

(Garth hands an apple to Anna. She stops to look at it.)

Anna: Garth, do you know what? This apple looks a little bit like a doll. I think I could make it into a doll.

(Anna sets down her basket. She sits down.)

Anna: Come, little doll. I will put two seeds here so you can see. Next I will put seeds over your chin so you can grin! Now here are sticks for your arms and your legs and feet. I think Mom will stitch a dress for you. I will ask for a hat to match! You will be my apple doll. The family will like you!

Garth: Anna, let's go home. It's getting dark.

(Anna takes the doll and Garth takes her basket. They run home.)

Setting: *The family cabin.*

Anna: Mom! Dad! Look what I made!

(The family looks at Anna's doll.)

Dad: Why, Anna! That's so good!

Charles: I like it! You made an apple doll!

Kip: I like what you did with the seeds!

Mitch: I like her feet!

Garth: I bet there is no doll like it in all the West!

Mom: Anna, your friends will want dolls like this. You can help them make apple dolls, too.

Anna: Yes! We can all have apple dolls. That will be fun!

Think About It

1. How does Anna make her doll?

2. What do Charles, Kip, and Mitch think of Anna before she makes her doll? How do you know?

3. Anna will make an apple doll to give to a friend. Make a card to go with the doll. What will the card look like? What will it say? Draw and write your ideas.

Auction Day

by Carol Storment
illustrated by Anthony Carnabuci

When Ty spied the pony in the pen of wild horses, he knew what he had to do. First he went to the bank.

"How much money do I have?" he asked.

The man smiled. "You're a rich man, Tyrone. You have six dollars."

"Is that enough for that pony outside?" asked Ty.

The man looked out the window. "Oh no, Ty. Those horses will go for ten dollars or more. Besides, what good would a wild pony be on a farm?"

Ty didn't say another word. He went across the road to the store. Ty had a plan to get his pony.

"Is there any work I could do for you, Mrs. Wyman?" Ty asked. "I need some extra money."

The storekeeper said, "Why yes, Tyrone. I'll find something for you to do."

Ty started by sweeping up. All morning he worked around the store, stacking shelves and cleaning the back room. When he was done, Mrs. Wyman gave him a dollar.

Ty walked by the pen full of wild horses. There she was, the littlest pony. Her coat was so black, it was almost blue. "Hello, Blue Sky," Ty said. He put out his hand. The shy pony jumped away. Her eyes were wild, but they looked sad, too.

"Be brave, girl!" Ty said. "You'll be out of here tomorrow."

The next day, Ty went to see three of his neighbors. He asked each one, "Is there work I can do for you?"

"You bet there is!" they all said.

First, Ty cut tall grass for Mr. Dyer. Then he moved a pile of rocks for Mr. Ryan. He fed chickens and collected eggs for Mrs. Bly. He worked until Mrs. Bly fried some eggs for his lunch. She asked Ty what he needed the money for.

"A pony" was all he would say. Then he went back to work. Ty tried his best to do each task well. He wanted his neighbors to be satisfied with his work.

When Ty was done, each neighbor was happy and paid him one dollar. Now he had three more dollars! The neighbors watched as he left for home. "That Tyrone works hard," they all agreed. "But he'll have his hands full if he tries to tame a wild pony!"

When Ty got home, he got out his bank. He counted all his money. Then he borrowed a horse and rode as fast as he could into town. He ran to the bank. It was still open.

"I'll take my six dollars, please," Ty told the man.

The man smiled. "Here you go. Good luck at the sale tomorrow!"

15

The sale started early. Everyone in the county came to see the wild horses. Ty was there with his money clutched in his hand.

The auctioneer called out that it was time to start. The bids began. The horses were going for much more than ten dollars. Ty felt like crying. He wouldn't have enough money!

At last only Blue Sky was left. Ty bid ten dollars. Everyone in town knew how much Ty wanted that pony. No one said a word.

"Sold!" shouted the auctioneer. "That pony is all yours, son."

All of Ty's neighbors clapped for him.

Ty and his family got Blue Sky home and into her new pen. Ty sat and watched her for a while. Her blue-black coat was glistening in the sun. Her mane was flying in the wind. But her eyes were still wild and sad. Then Ty got up and opened the gate. Blue Sky shot out and galloped away.

His father ran up. "Ty! Why did you let the pony get away? You worked so hard to get the money for her!"

Ty said, "Blue Sky would never be happy living on a farm. I was glad to spend my money to set her free."

Ty felt proud as his pony galloped to freedom. *Fly away, Blue Sky!*

Think About It

1. What does Ty do so that he can buy Blue Sky?

2. Why do you think Ty doesn't tell anyone he plans to set Blue Sky free?

3. Write the diary entry Ty might write the day he lets Blue Sky go.

THE RACE TO THE SEA

Story by Kaye Gager

Illustrations by Donna Delich

The beach has a secret. Mom said so.
I look and look for the secret. I look in
a wet log. I get up on a big rock. I am
eager to see the secret. What can it be?

I wish I could dig for it. Mom said no
digging at all. That could be bad.

Mom said we can collect litter. I find weird
junk, but I do not find the secret. I run down
to the big rock. The red sun sets over the sea.
We will have to look tomorrow.

The sun is setting when I run down to the beach. Mom runs with me. When we get there, there are fishing ships dancing on the sea. But what is the secret?

Mom gets up on the big rock. I get up with her. We are eager, but we have to sit patiently.

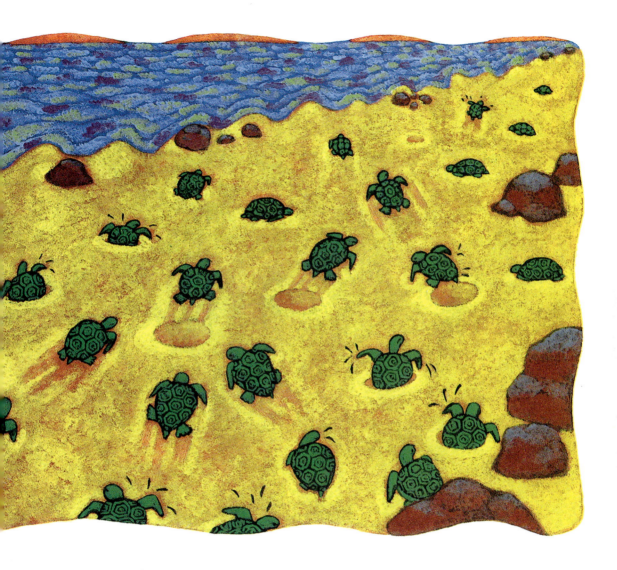

Then I see something. I see something digging! Then I see digging all over the beach.

There they are! Is this the secret? My mom nods. They look weird. Sand is all over them. What are they going to do?

Then they run. Look at that speed! They run for the sea. It looks as if they have trained for it. Are they going to make it?

No! Look up there! A sea gull is going to get one of them! It misses. Mom and I clap and clap.

"Come on!" I yell to them. "You have to get to the sea!" They run down the beach to the rocks. The sea gives them a bath. The sand comes off them as they swim. Then the little swimmers go out to sea.

They are like friends now! I will be sad not to see them at the beach tomorrow.

What are they going to do now? That is a secret of the wise sea. I wish I could get a message to them.

I look at the sea and wish them well. The sea gulls can not find them now. My little friends are dancing in the sea. They are swimming in the sun. The sea gulls will have to have fish!

26

Think About It

1. What secret does the beach have?

2. Why do you think the boy's mom does not tell him what the secret is?

3. Make a postcard from the boy in the story to a friend. Draw a picture on one side to show the secret. Write a message on the other side that tells about it.

A Troublesome NOSE

by Linda Lott   illustrated by Russ Wilson

Miss Jones's class is planning a holiday pageant. Ron is glad that they are going to act out his favorite book.

In the book, a fox, a dog, and a frog make a visit to a tropical land. They plan a fine holiday, but troublesome problems come up.

Ron hopes to get a role, and he is not disappointed.
He gets to be the fox. He has the greatest lines—they're
all jokes. All the kids like the fox.

Ron says his lines over and over so he will not make
a mistake on stage. His mom and dad will be coming
to the pageant.

The time comes for the dress rehearsal, and Miss Jones
gives out the costumes. Ron's is a fake fox nose.

The long nose looks fine, but it's a troublesome nose. The problem is that it flip-flops up and down. It flips up, and Ron can't see. It flops down, and it's over his lips. When Ron says his lines, all that comes out is "Mmm, mmm, mmm." The kids can't get the jokes.

Ron jogs home, swinging the nose on its string. When he gets inside, Mom looks up.

"What a fine nose!" she says.

"It's not fine at all," Ron says. He pops the nose on and says his lines. The nose flip-flops up and down. Mom can't get anything but "Mmm, mmm, mmm."

Dad grins and hands Ron some tape. "You'll have to fix it so it doesn't flip-flop," he says.

"I hope I can fix it in time," Ron says.

At the pageant, it's time for the fox to be seen. Ron lopes onto the stage. All the kids smile.

Mom and Dad gaze attentively at the nose. What if it still slips? Can Ron cope with it?

The nose does slip! First it rides up so Ron can't see. Ron gropes for it, and the kids all grin. Then the nose slips down over Ron's lips.

"Mmm, mmm, mmm," says the fox.

The kids are having a fit. Ron grins back at them. Then he puts the nose up on top. Now he can say his lines just fine. He does not make one mistake.

Mom and Dad clap and clap. Then they make a visit to the stage.

"Good job, Ron!" they say. "You came up with a fine solution to your problem."

"I like that fox role," says Ron. "The jokes are all good ones. The troublesome nose was the greatest joke of all!"

Think About It

1. What is Ron's role in the holiday pageant? Why does he like that role?

2. Why is the big nose the greatest joke of all?

3. After the play, Ron writes a postcard to his friend. He tells all about the troublesome nose. Write the postcard Ron sends.

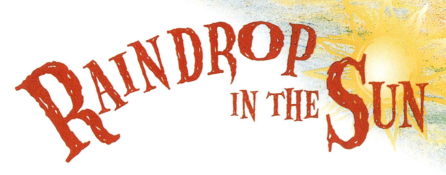

RAINDROP IN THE SUN

by Deborah Akers   **illustrated by Miles Hyman**

Moro said Lani couldn't go with the men to gather abalones.

"Lani, you are a girl. How could you paddle a canoe? Also, these shells are very hard to get off a rock. You must be strong for this work."

Moro gave Lani a fierce look. Then he strode off to the canoes. There was no more to be said.

Lani was sad. She was also mad.

"I *am* strong. I could paddle a canoe. I could get the abalones off the rocks, too."

36

People from the tribe gathered on the shore.
Lani and her mother watched the canoes set out.
Lani looked forlorn.

Before Kalo, Lani's brother, got in his canoe,
he gave her a hug. "It's not fair, is it?"

"No! I could help you bring home more meat,"
Lani said.

"Do you think you could?" Kalo gave his sister a
hard look. Then he whispered, "Meet me over at the
entrance to the cove. I will hide you in my canoe."

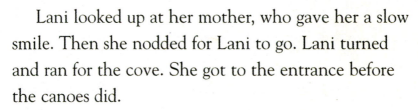

Lani looked up at her mother, who gave her a slow smile. Then she nodded for Lani to go. Lani turned and ran for the cove. She got to the entrance before the canoes did.

When Kalo pulled up, Lani leaped into his canoe. She curled up on the bottom so no one could see her.

Kalo paddled hard. Then he floated the canoe into a rock shelter.

"We need to look low on the rocks for big shells. The big ones will have more meat," he said.

They came to some rocks with lots of seals perched on them. The seals sat in their lair and gorged on fish. They sunned themselves and admired their sleek coats. One big fellow, vainer than the rest, licked his fur all over.

Kalo and Lani smiled at each other and paddled on. Past the seals' lair, they discovered rocks with big abalones stuck to them. They lost no time in getting to work.

Kalo would grab a shell, and Lani would scrape it
off with the paddle. Together they made a good team.
They were quick workers, and before long they had a
big load.

"We should be getting home now," said Kalo.
"The waves are getting big."

In no time a fierce storm was upon them. They
could see the other canoes coming their way. Then
a gigantic wave flipped all those canoes over!

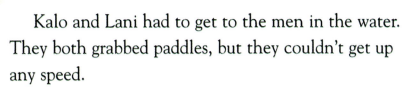

Kalo and Lani had to get to the men in the water. They both grabbed paddles, but they couldn't get up any speed.

"Throw the abalones over the side!" yelled Kalo. "They're making us too slow!"

Lani pitched all the shells but one. When they got to the canoes, Lani reached out with her paddle. She turned each one right side up. Kalo pulled Moro from the water, and the two of them helped the other men. Then they all paddled for shelter.

At last they were safe on shore. Mama and the others ran out to meet them.

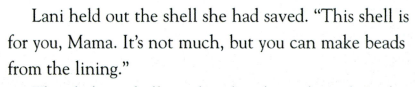

Lani held out the shell she had saved. "This shell is for you, Mama. It's not much, but you can make beads from the lining."

The abalone shell was lined with mother-of-pearl. Deep inside the meat, there was something more. It was something not one of them had ever seen—an abalone pearl. Its colors shone like a raindrop in the sun.

Moro strode forward and spoke. He said the pearl was a trophy for their hero, Lani. Mama was overcome when Moro talked of how Lani and Kalo had saved the men. She was so glad to have her strong, brave girl safe at home again.

Think About It

1. Why does Moro say Lani can't go with the men to gather abalones?

2. Why do you think Kalo takes his sister along to gather abalones? How do you think he feels when the fierce storm comes up?

3. The next time the men go out to gather abalones, Lani and some other girls ask to go along. Write what you think they say and what the men tell them.

43

ROOM to SHARE

written by Julio Mendez
illustrated by Sandy Appleoff

Mike woke up and smiled. His grandpa was coming. That was the good news. Then Mom gave Mike the bad news.

"Make your room look good," Mom said. "Make room for Grandpa Ike, too. He'll be your roommate."

Mike sat right up. This was unexpected. Mike liked his grandpa, but he liked his room, too. It was all his. It was where he went when his baby sisters acted like pests.

"Mom," Mike griped. "My room is tiny. It's just the right size for me."

Mike's mom glanced over at Mike.

"In this family, we share," she said.

Mike longed for the comfort of a room for himself, but he said, "OK, Mom. I'll do it for the family."

"Thanks, Mike," Mom said. "That's fine."

She left for work, where she filled prescriptions.

When his grandpa came, Mike smiled
and hugged him. At the same time, he was
thinking about sharing his room.

"I know I'll like being your roommate,"
Grandpa Ike said.

"Me, too," said Mike, but he could not
look at his grandpa.

"We'll have a good time," Grandpa
Ike went on. "Just the two of us."

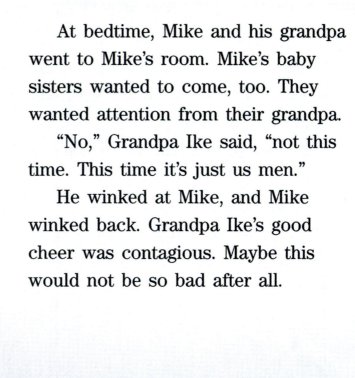

At bedtime, Mike and his grandpa went to Mike's room. Mike's baby sisters wanted to come, too. They wanted attention from their grandpa.

"No," Grandpa Ike said, "not this time. This time it's just us men."

He winked at Mike, and Mike winked back. Grandpa Ike's good cheer was contagious. Maybe this would not be so bad after all.

In Mike's room, Grandpa Ike unpacked his suitcase. He pulled out a wide blanket and made a tent with it.

"Here we are in Camp Mike and Ike," he said.

Then he pulled out a tiny TV.

"We may be camping," he said, "but we still like the comforts of home."

Then Grandpa Ike got out a pile of snacks. He cut some pie for Mike.

"Now I'll tell you a family story," he said. "I'll tell you what your mom was like when she was nine. She was quite a bit like your baby sisters."

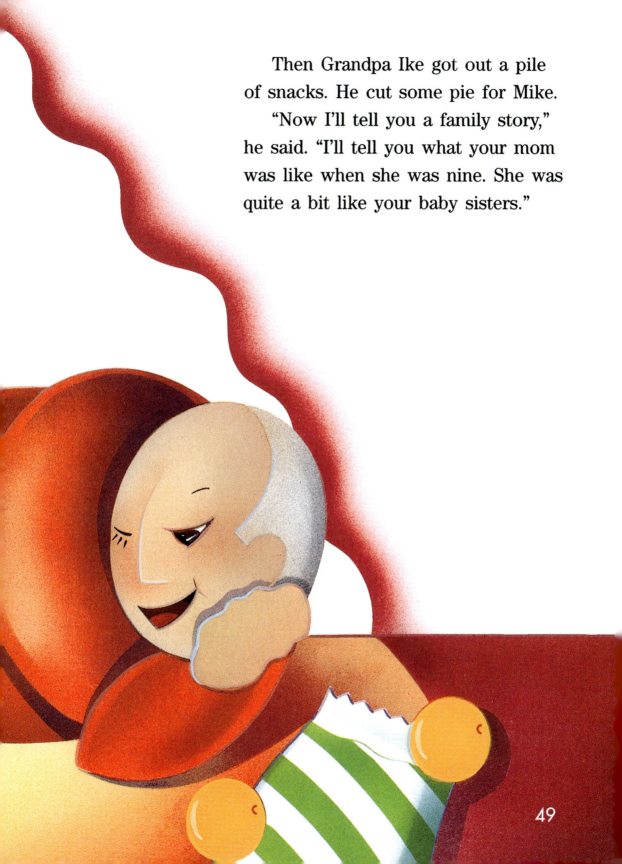

Mike had fun. He and his grandpa giggled and laughed. The time went by fast. Mike got very tired. He got into the top bunk to lie down.

Grandpa Ike said, "I like this, but it's too bad you have to share your room."

Mike smiled a wide smile.

"That's all right," he said. "There's room enough to share, and you are a fine roommate."

Think About It

1. How does Grandpa Ike make having a roommate fun for Mike?

2. Why can't Mike look at Grandpa when he says "Me, too"?

3. After Grandpa Ike goes home, he will write Mike a thank-you note. Write the note he might send.

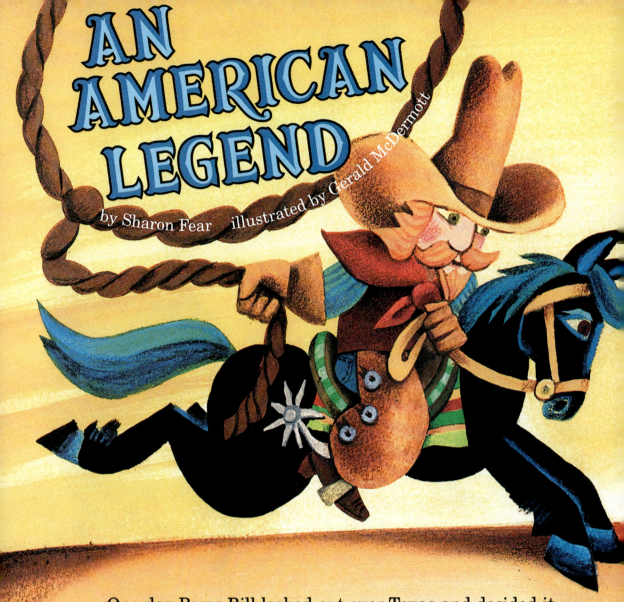

AN AMERICAN LEGEND

by Sharon Fear   illustrated by Gerald McDermott

One day Pecos Bill looked out over Texas and decided it was time to move on.

True, Texas had given him plenty from the time he was a little bitty baby. Hadn't the coyotes of Texas taken him in and raised him when he got bumped off his parents' wagon?

But Bill had repaid Texas. Hadn't he created the cowboy life, holding the first roundup and inventing the lariat and other gadgets?

52

Hadn't he tamed all the Texas tornadoes by riding them into the ground? Why, a stampeding herd of thirsty giant mosquitoes was about the only trouble left in Texas!

That was the problem. Texas was just too tame for the untamed spirit of Pecos Bill.

"I reckon we'll head west," Bill said to his horse, "and set up a brand-new ranch."

Bill went and claimed some land called New Mexico that he figured would do for his new ranch. Then he said to his horse, "I reckon we'll need cowhands."

Bill asked around. "I need men who are rough, tough, untamed, impolite, and disagreeable! In other words, real cowboys!"

"There's a wild bunch fitting all your requirements right up that canyon," said an old-timer.

"Much obliged!" said Bill. He tipped his ten-gallon hat and off he rode.

On the way up the canyon, Bill's horse got spooked. It bucked off Bill and his saddle and headed for home. Right in Bill's path was a rattlesnake of impossible size!

Old softhearted Bill let the snake have the first bite. Then he hollered, "Enough of this nonsense! I'm Pecos Bill, and you're a snake sandwich!"

Bill jumped on the rattler, tied it in knots, and flung it around his neck. "I was needing a new whip to crack," he said, very pleased.

55

Just then a wildcat of impossible size sprang upon Bill and tried to chew his head off.

Bill was rather annoyed. He jumped up, bellowing, "I'm Pecos Bill, and you're a wildcat sandwich!"

This might have meant tragedy for the cat, but with his horse gone, Bill needed something to ride. Before that wildcat knew what was happening, Bill threw his saddle on it and jumped aboard. He rode that cat, bucking and screeching, till it was meek as a kitten.

"Thanks," said Bill. "I enjoyed that."

Bill rode on until he saw some men boiling up beans
and coffee over a campfire. They were as big as grizzlies
and twice as mean-looking. That may have been because
they were surrounded by swirling clouds of mosquitoes.
Bill cracked his rattlesnake whip, and the pesky critters
hightailed it out of there.

"Howdy, boys," said Bill. "I'm mighty hungry and
thirsty. How about a ration of that grub?"

He reached into the boiling beans, grabbed some, and
gobbled them. He tipped up the coffeepot and swigged
down the boiling brew.

"Now, boys," he said, wiping his chin with a prickly pear
cactus, "who's boss around here?"

They looked at the man who rode a wildcat, cracked a rattlesnake whip, swallowed boiling grub, and used a cactus for a napkin. Those cowpokes knew that this was a fateful moment for them.

"You are!" they said.

From then on those boys were as loyal as puppies to Bill. They helped him set up one ranch and then moved on with him to another. Just as the legends about Pecos Bill endure, so, too, that ranch endures to this day.

It's called Arizona.

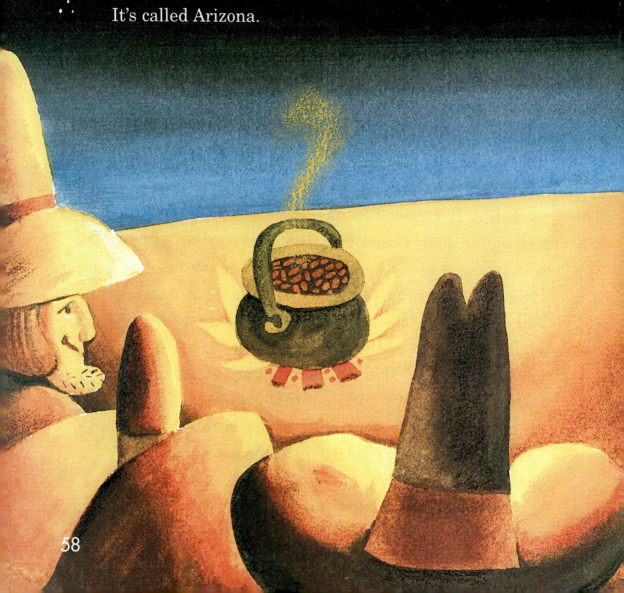

Think About It

1. Why do the wild bunch of men agree to work for Pecos Bill?

2. How do you think the rattlesnake feels when it first sees Pecos Bill? How do you think it feels when he says, "I was needing a new whip to crack"?

3. Choose one of the things Pecos Bill does before he leaves Texas. Write your own story about how Pecos Bill does that.

Fire in the

by Caren B. Stelson   illustrated by Carmelo Blandino

Remember Smokey Bear, the forest ranger's best friend? Smokey always said it was everyone's job to take care of the forest. He said, "Only YOU can prevent forest fires." That's still true, but times have changed.

Forest rangers no longer believe that all fires are bad. In fact, rangers now think that some fires may even be good for a forest.

Forest

Since leaping flames destroy trees, you might ask, "How can a fire be good for a forest?" It seems that fire is the way a forest renews itself.

Fire burns old branches, underbrush, and diseased trees. The ashes from these make the soil richer, and more sunlight reaches the forest floor. This leads to fast growth of strong, new trees. Today, forest rangers think of fire as an important part of a forest's life cycle.

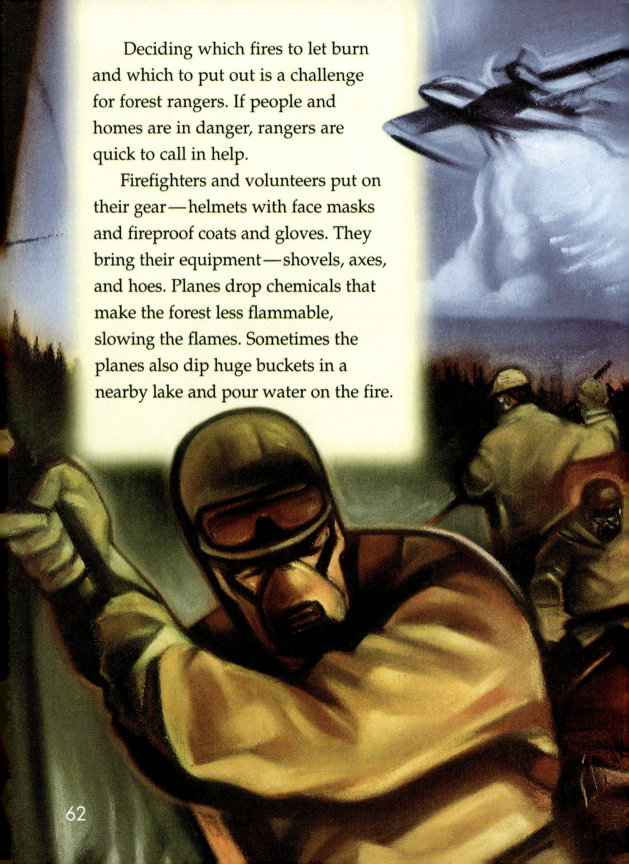

Deciding which fires to let burn and which to put out is a challenge for forest rangers. If people and homes are in danger, rangers are quick to call in help.

Firefighters and volunteers put on their gear—helmets with face masks and fireproof coats and gloves. They bring their equipment—shovels, axes, and hoes. Planes drop chemicals that make the forest less flammable, slowing the flames. Sometimes the planes also dip huge buckets in a nearby lake and pour water on the fire.

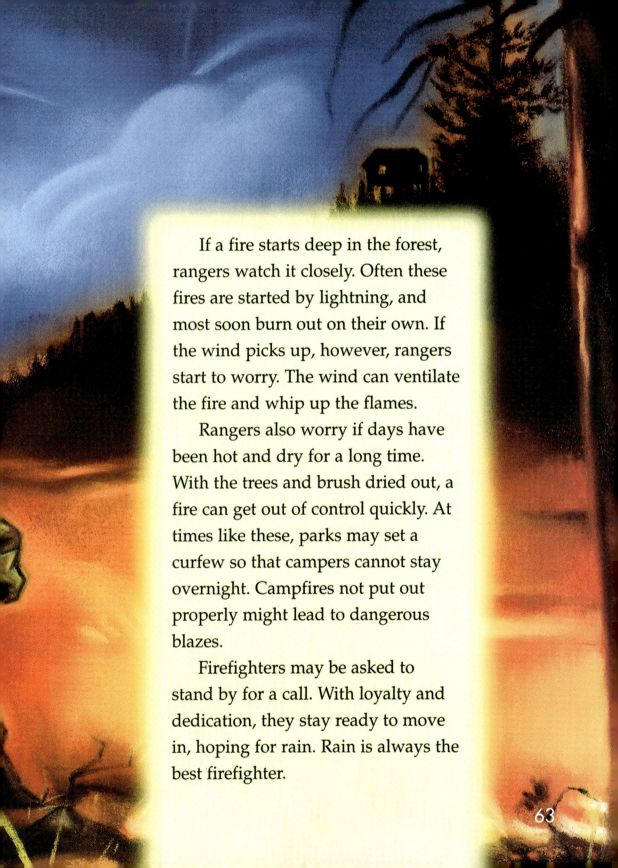

If a fire starts deep in the forest, rangers watch it closely. Often these fires are started by lightning, and most soon burn out on their own. If the wind picks up, however, rangers start to worry. The wind can ventilate the fire and whip up the flames.

Rangers also worry if days have been hot and dry for a long time. With the trees and brush dried out, a fire can get out of control quickly. At times like these, parks may set a curfew so that campers cannot stay overnight. Campfires not put out properly might lead to dangerous blazes.

Firefighters may be asked to stand by for a call. With loyalty and dedication, they stay ready to move in, hoping for rain. Rain is always the best firefighter.

In 1988, rangers faced a serious fire challenge in Yellowstone National Park. It was a hot summer, and the forest was extremely dry. There had been little snow that year, and it had hardly rained at all for six weeks.

When lightning started fires deep in the forest, rangers decided it was safe to let them burn. Then the wind picked up, and everything changed. Flames 200 feet tall leaped and roared. They started new fires and rekindled old ones.

The strong winds sent smoke billowing over the park. Visitors and cabins were now at risk. Firefighters from many cities arrived with their equipment. Brigades of volunteers put on firefighting gear, too. All joined forces, but each time they seemed to have the blaze under control, it rekindled.

The fires raged all summer. Finally, in September, it started to rain, and the fires at last sputtered out. Millions of trees had been lost, but the forest itself had not been destroyed. By the next summer, a new carpet of grass and millions of wildflowers covered the hillsides. The forest had started to heal. The cycle of life had begun once again.

Think About It

1. Why do forest rangers allow some fires to burn?

2. Why is it still important for people to prevent forest fires?

3. You are a trained firefighter who has spent a long day fighting a forest fire. Write a letter home, telling what you have done.

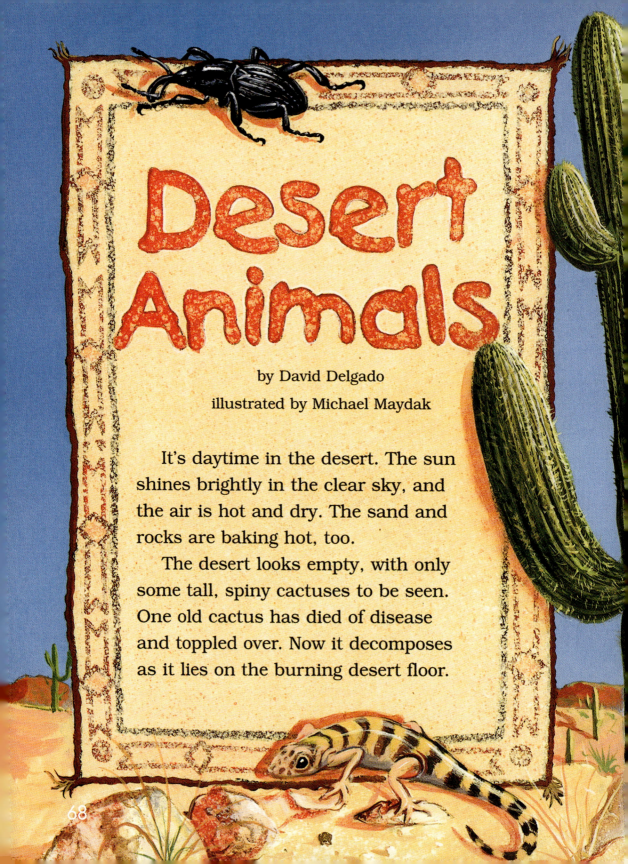

Desert Animals

by David Delgado

illustrated by Michael Maydak

It's daytime in the desert. The sun shines brightly in the clear sky, and the air is hot and dry. The sand and rocks are baking hot, too.

The desert looks empty, with only some tall, spiny cactuses to be seen. One old cactus has died of disease and toppled over. Now it decomposes as it lies on the burning desert floor.

Scrubby bushes grow in the desert, too. The low branches of this brush offer desert creatures a little shade from the hot sunlight.

At first sight, the desert doesn't seem to be the habitat of many creatures. If you take a closer look, however, you'll see that many kinds of animals live in the desert. These animals have adapted to the harsh, dry climate. They can live where many other animals could not survive.

If you stir up the sand, you may find that it is teeming with life. Many insects, such as ants, beetles, and even bees, dig burrows. Staying underground protects the bugs from the blazing sun.

The digger bee makes a long, narrow tunnel beneath the sand. Here it stores pollen for food and lays a single egg. The baby bee will spend many months growing safely underground.

If you look in the shade under the brush, you may see a lizard trying to keep cool. It has climbed up onto a branch to get away from the heat of the ground. The zebra–tailed lizard sometimes runs on its back feet across the open desert. It does this to keep its front feet and body up off the hot sand.

Plodding along nearby is a big, slow-moving reptile that looks like a land-dwelling turtle. The animal's shell protects it from the sun's hot rays. It gets the water it needs from the plants it eats. One of its favorite foods is cactus flowers.

Take another look at the desert. It's far from empty—in fact, it's almost crowded!

You may spy a rattlesnake asleep in the shade of a rock. Rattlers rest during the heat of the day and come out to hunt and eat at night.

The jackrabbit has big ears that help keep it from getting too hot. They provide more skin to let off extra body heat.

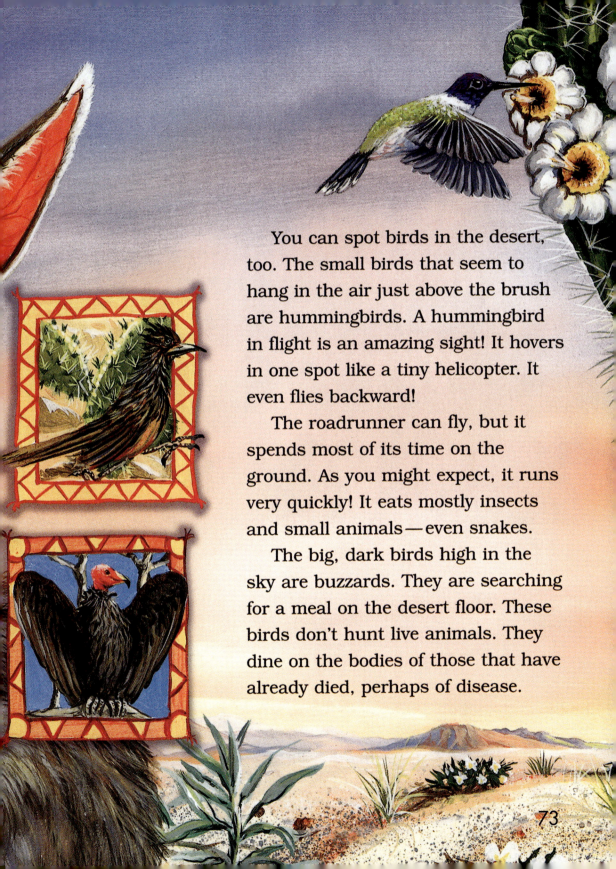

You can spot birds in the desert, too. The small birds that seem to hang in the air just above the brush are hummingbirds. A hummingbird in flight is an amazing sight! It hovers in one spot like a tiny helicopter. It even flies backward!

The roadrunner can fly, but it spends most of its time on the ground. As you might expect, it runs very quickly! It eats mostly insects and small animals—even snakes.

The big, dark birds high in the sky are buzzards. They are searching for a meal on the desert floor. These birds don't hunt live animals. They dine on the bodies of those that have already died, perhaps of disease.

When night comes, the desert is almost crowded. Some different creatures are awake now, after the heat of the day.

Insects buzz through the air, and bats fly out to dine on the insects. Coyotes prowl far and wide, hunting snakes, lizards, birds, and smaller mammals. The lonely howl of the coyote is the night song of the desert.

Day and night, the desert is alive with animals.

Think About It

1. What is the main problem for animals in the desert?

2. Why is it sometimes hard to see animals in the desert?

3. Choose one desert animal. What else would you like to know about that animal? Write four questions you want to have answered.

Frontier

by Kana Riley

The sun rises over a sea of grass that stretches in endless waves across the plains. The light wakes the children and they crawl out from under their comfortable quilts and dress quickly. It is time to do the chores.

At first the children yawn and blink sleepily. Outside their sod home, however, their energy is restored by the fresh air, and they shiver in the early morning chill. Fall comes early in this climate, and soon the grass will be covered with snow.

Children

The girl grabs a milk pail and a three-legged stool. Her designated chore is to milk the cow that waits in the small barn. Like the house, the barn is made of chunks of sod cut from the grassland.

The girl's younger brother tosses handfuls of corn to the chickens and then feeds the mule. The hungry animals crowd around him trustingly.

Both children work quickly because today is a school day, and they don't want to be late. They will be sorry when snow blocks the road to the schoolhouse. Then they will have to stay home.

Children living on farms today are still expected to be capable helpers.

The climate of the plains is often harsh. In winter the snow-covered plains can seem empty and desolate.

This will be the family's second winter on the plains. Two summers ago they crossed the country in a wagon train as part of the great exodus from the East. Hundreds of families migrated to the West to find good farming land.

When they got to their land, it seemed to the children a useless and desolate place—not a single tree grew anywhere. Their father had dug a hole into the side of a hill, the way a burrowing animal does. He had walled up the open

side, and that's where they had spent the first winter.

Their home back East had been in a town. The children didn't know if they'd like homesteading in a community where friends and farms were miles apart.

Finally spring came, and the family set to work to construct a proper house. In other parts of the frontier, people lived in adobe houses or log cabins. On the plains, there was no clay for making adobe bricks, and there were no trees to provide logs for a cabin. The new home would be a "soddy," built of bricks cut from the sod.

As soon as the sod home was finished, the family turned to planting crops. The parents plowed the land, and the children planted seeds and hauled water.

In the fall the whole family harvested the crops. They put some foods aside for winter and sold the rest in town. They earned enough money to pay the first installment on the loan they had taken for the land.

Some farmers still use horse-drawn plows to cut through sod.

"Breakfast!" the children's mother calls. This morning it's homemade bread and jam. The girl smiles, remembering the pailful of berries she collected to make the jam.

Their mother puts a hard-boiled egg in each of their lunch pails. "Fresh from your chickens," the boy's father says to him with a smile.

The girl helps her brother onto the mule and climbs up behind him. Riding to school is certainly better than walking!

At the schoolhouse, children are playing Snap-the-Whip before school begins. They have formed a long line, holding hands. The leader pulls the line in fast turns, trying to make those on the end lose their grip.

The girl and boy join in the friendly game. Running and shouting with their new friends, they forget how desolate this homesteading community once seemed to them. Now it is home.

One teacher taught children of all ages who attended this one-room sod schoolhouse.

Think About It

1. How is the family's frontier house different from their old house?

2. How do you think the girl and boy feel about doing their chores?

3. The girl sends a letter to a friend back in the town her family left. She tells her friend about her new life on the plains. Write the letter the girl sends.

Bringing Back the
PUFFINS

by Caren B. Stelson
illustrated by Paul Mirocha

Spring has come back to Egg Rock, but will the puffins come back too? A man named Steve Kress watches and hopes. For a long time, no puffins had nested on these uninhabited rocks. Then Kress started a plan to bring them back. He hopes his puffin plan will go right.

Over 100 years ago, puffins nested on Egg Rock. Kress wanted to see them there again. In 1973, he and his team went to a land that has many puffins. They collected puffin chicks, being very careful with them, and then rushed them back to Egg Rock.

Steve Kress and his team acted as parents to tend the puffin chicks. They made a village of burrows for the chicks to nestle in. They fed them fresh fish and kept them safe from dangers, such as gulls. Kress and his team made good puffin parents!

One night the puffins came out of their village of burrows. It was time for them to venture into the sea. Each made a wobbling flight, splashed in, and went out into the dark night.

Would the puffins come back to breed and to tend their chicks? Kress hoped that in two to three years, they would instinctively do this.

There are many dangers for puffins at sea. They can be eaten if a gull spies them. They can be stranded in fishing nets. They can be harmed by big waves.

Yet puffins are made for sea life. They can dive deep and swim fast. They use their wings to swim and their webbed feet to steer. They catch fish with their sharp beaks. Kress hoped at least some of his puffins would make it back to Egg Rock.

Now Steve Kress sits on Egg Rock, keeping watch and hoping his plan was not just a dream. He watches for a long, long time.

Then Kress spies a black speck in flight. The speck gets bigger and bigger as it sweeps over the sea. Kress leaps to his feet and yells to his team. The puffins have come back to Egg Rock!

Think About It

1. How did Steve Kress and his team help puffin chicks live on Egg Rock?

2. Why did the adult puffins come back to Egg Rock?

3. What else do you want to know about puffins? Write three questions you would like to ask Steve Kress.

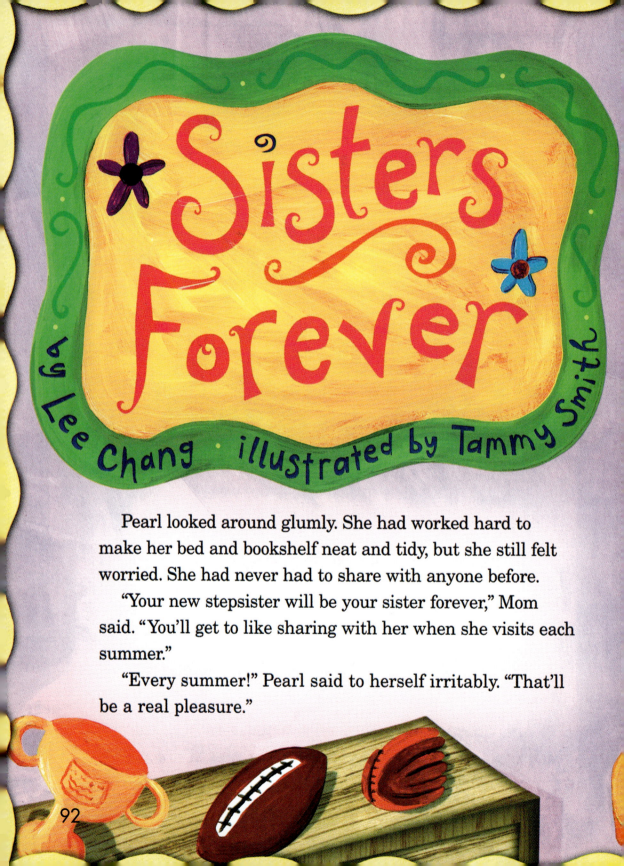

Sisters Forever

by Lee Chang · illustrated by Tammy Smith

Pearl looked around glumly. She had worked hard to make her bed and bookshelf neat and tidy, but she still felt worried. She had never had to share with anyone before.

"Your new stepsister will be your sister forever," Mom said. "You'll get to like sharing with her when she visits each summer."

"Every summer!" Pearl said to herself irritably. "That'll be a real pleasure."

All the way to the airport to meet LaVerne's plane, Pearl tried to ignore the situation. She was just getting used to having a stepfather, and now she had to get used to having a stepsister, too.

When LaVerne walked off the plane, Pearl gave her a weak smile. LaVerne wore her curly hair long with a bow. Pearl kept her hair short for sports. LaVerne looked like a girl with very different interests from hers. How would the two of them ever get along?

93

Pearl did not feel more hopeful when her stepsister unpacked her things. First LaVerne put a stuffed toy cat next to Pearl's baseball mitt. Then she cluttered the tidy shelf with her books and the rest of her possessions.

Pearl's disposition changed. She didn't feel happy anymore. She felt that LaVerne was imposing on her. Pearl didn't want to be mean, but she couldn't help feeling a grudge.

LaVerne seemed no happier with the situation than Pearl. At dinner, the girls started to bicker. They both looked angry and sad.

Pearl's stepfather tried to cheer them up. "This summer will be fun," he said. "I like having my two girls together. I wouldn't be surprised if you find you like some of the same pastimes."

The girls just frowned and looked down at their plates. They had to be sisters forever, but they didn't have to like it.

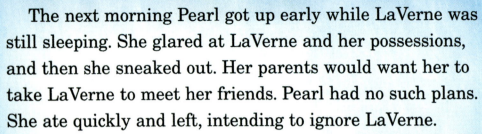

The next morning Pearl got up early while LaVerne was still sleeping. She glared at LaVerne and her possessions, and then she sneaked out. Her parents would want her to take LaVerne to meet her friends. Pearl had no such plans. She ate quickly and left, intending to ignore LaVerne.

Pearl played soccer with her friends all morning. At lunchtime she went home feeling bad. Sneaking out on LaVerne had been mean. Now Mom might make her stay home all afternoon and play with LaVerne and her stuffed toys.

When Pearl reached her yard, she was surprised to find LaVerne kicking a soccer ball around.

"I didn't know you liked sports," Pearl said. "You brought so many books with you, I figured you just liked to read."

"I do like to read," LaVerne said, "but I have other interests, too. At home, I play sports every day."

"I like sports," Pearl said, "and I like to read, too. At school I tutor the first graders in reading."

"You can read my books if you want to," said LaVerne. "Do you like to play board games?"

"Yes, I do," said Pearl. "I guess your dad was right. We *do* have some pastimes we both like."

"I guess parents can be right once in a while," LaVerne joked, and they both laughed.

For the first time, the girls gave each other a real smile. The situation was not so bad after all. It began to look as if being sisters forever *could* turn out to be a real pleasure.

Think About It

1. Why does Pearl have to share with LaVerne?

2. Why does Pearl think LaVerne doesn't like sports?

3. Think about Pearl and LaVerne. Write one paragraph telling how the two girls are the same. Write another paragraph telling how they are different.

BLIZZARD SEASON

by Kaye Gager   illustrated by Karen Pritchett

When I woke up, I could tell right away there was a problem. No sunshine came in, and blasts of wind were shaking the cabin.

I got up and looked outdoors. A blizzard, of all things! How could this be? It was the middle of May! When we went to bed, it was springtime.

I got the children up and helped them dress. Ma bustled around, making us a pot of hot tea with honey. We all sat near the stove with our mugs.

"Children," Ma said, "this is a big storm. We'll have to do our chores when it lets up a bit. Pa will be back this afternoon, but that could be too late!"

"How can we be having a blizzard, Ma?" I asked. "It's May and all my plants are up!"

Ma said, "Sometimes we do have a spring storm. You children just haven't seen one. Your plants may be all right, Bess."

When the snow stopped for a while, we did our chores frantically. Jen and Jeff dug a path to the hens. Little Tim held the sack of feed. Ma and I dragged some cut logs inside by the stove.

All the while, I was thinking of my hidden plants. I hoped the deep snow was not freezing their new little stems and leaves.

In no time, the blizzard was back. Stinging snow scoured our cheeks and noses.

Ma staggered over to me.

"Bess, get the children," she said. "It's time to stop. We did what we could."

We were thankful to be inside our snug home. Ma got out her flute, and we sang all our favorite tunes. In the afternoon Pa made it home safe from his trip.

By the time we went to bed, the blizzard was over. Just a gentle breeze ruffled the snow.

When we got up, it was very still outdoors. Pa
and I did the chores while Ma made us a hot meal.
We ate it by the stove as the children ran around
restlessly.

"Can we go outdoors? It's not bad out there
now," Jen said earnestly.

Ma looked out. "You can go, but you must keep
your hats on!"

We put on our outdoor things fast, hats and all.
Little Tim looked so cute in his hat with kitten ears!

We had the greatest time outside! We waded in
the deep snow. We slipped and slid. We pulled Tim in
a box and made snow people. Jen and I hid, and
when Jeff came near, we pelted him with snow. That
gave him an excuse to get us! Whap!

Then Tim said, "Look! There's the sun!" We looked
up. Tim was right!

By afternoon, the sun was hot. Our snow people melted, but we were glad to have spring back. There was mud all over, but the breeze smelled fresh.

Ma came out. "Spring storms come and go fast," she said, "but this one was amazing."

Then she said, "Look down, Bess!" I did, and there in the mud were green sprouts, green stems, and green leaves! Ma was right. My plants didn't freeze after all.

I gave Ma a big hug. It was May, and it would be June next. I hoped earnestly that blizzard season was over!

Think About It

1. What makes the storm so amazing?

2. Why hasn't Bess seen a spring storm before?

3. Make a web with words that tell what the main character, Bess, likes and what she does. Use the web to write a paragraph about Bess.

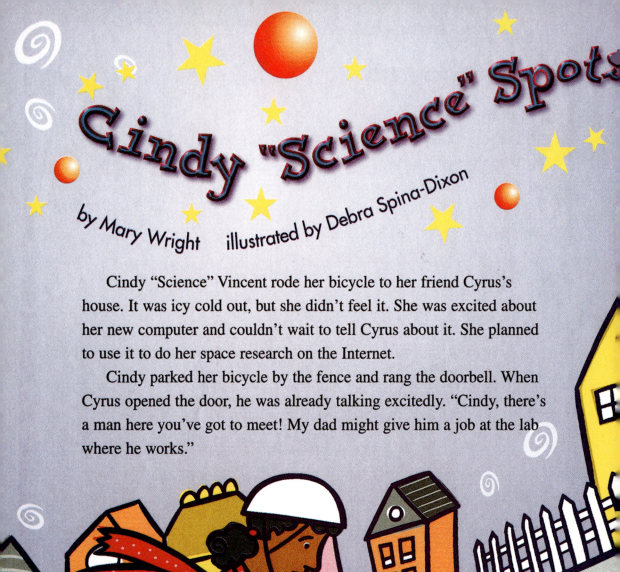

Cindy "Science" Spots

by Mary Wright   illustrated by Debra Spina-Dixon

Cindy "Science" Vincent rode her bicycle to her friend Cyrus's house. It was icy cold out, but she didn't feel it. She was excited about her new computer and couldn't wait to tell Cyrus about it. She planned to use it to do her space research on the Internet.

Cindy parked her bicycle by the fence and rang the doorbell. When Cyrus opened the door, he was already talking excitedly. "Cindy, there's a man here you've got to meet! My dad might give him a job at the lab where he works."

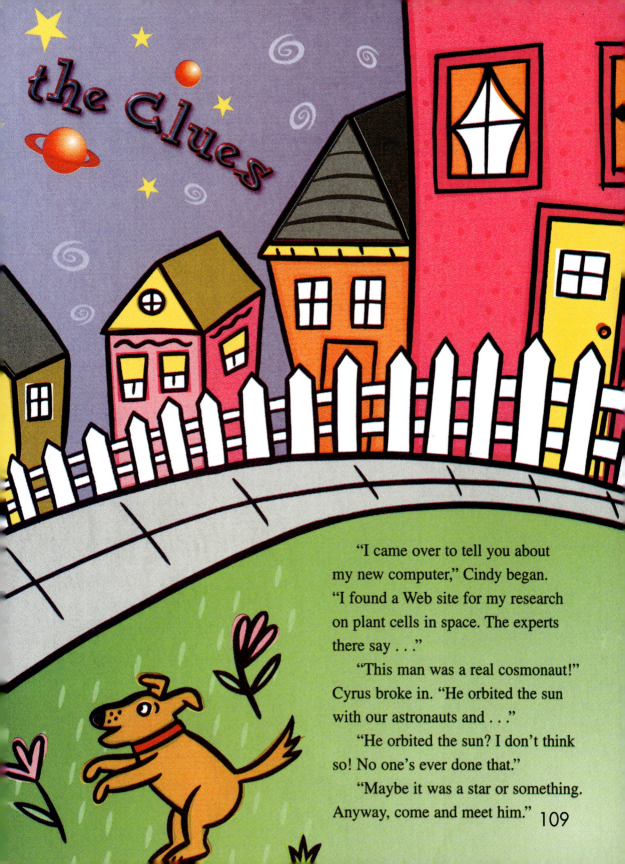

the Clues

"I came over to tell you about my new computer," Cindy began. "I found a Web site for my research on plant cells in space. The experts there say . . ."

"This man was a real cosmonaut!" Cyrus broke in. "He orbited the sun with our astronauts and . . ."

"He orbited the sun? I don't think so! No one's ever done that."

"Maybe it was a star or something. Anyway, come and meet him." 109

Inside, Cindy met Professor Durak, standing in the center of the family room. "Pleased to meet you, Cindy," he said. "I was just talking about the breakthrough I made for space science back in 1969."

Cyrus's dad smiled. "Cindy is an expert on space science, Professor Durak. She plans to make it her career."

"She enrolls in Space Camp every summer," Cyrus put in.

John Glenn Neil
Armstrong
Buzz Aldrin
Thanks for all your
help, Prof. July, 1999

Professor Durak gave Cindy a sharp look. "The experts disregarded my formulas in planning our flight. I had to teach things to the astronauts during the launch itself! They were so grateful, they signed this shirt for me right after the flight."

"What happened with the launch?" Cyrus asked.

"The spacecraft didn't take off properly," said Professor Durak. "The astronauts had no idea what to do, but of course I did.

"Our craft rose very quickly

through the atmosphere. The altimeter numbers went up faster
and faster. We passed a satellite on our way up. Once we had
left Earth's atmosphere, ah, that was a sight to see."

"What was?" Cindy asked.

"Seeing the planets from space, of course. Mars, the red
planet. Jupiter, with its ring. Venus, with its Great Red Spot.
Now, that was something!"

112

"Cyrus," Cindy broke in. "Can I get something to eat? Maybe some cereal or a slice of pie?"

Cyrus frowned, but Cindy dragged him into the kitchen anyway. "Professor Durak is a fake, Cyrus!" she said. "I hope your father hasn't given him a job."

Cyrus sighed dejectedly. "You always know what you're talking about, Cindy, so you're probably right. But how do you know Professor Durak's a fake?"

113

"There are two clues. First, look closely at the professor's shirt. Next, read about Jupiter."

Can YOU spot Professor Durak's mistakes? Look at the date on his shirt. Then check out Jupiter in a book or online.

Answer: The professor said his flight was in 1969, but the date on his shirt is 1999. The Great Red Spot is on Jupiter. It's an immense hurricane that was first seen in 1664. John Glenn, Neil Armstrong, and Buzz Aldrin were never on a mission together.

Think About It

1. Why does Cindy say that she hopes Cyrus's father has not given Professor Durak a job?

2. How do you think Professor Durak feels about meeting Cindy?

3. Think about Cindy "Science" Vincent. Make a web with words that tell about her interests and the things she does. Then write a paragraph describing Cindy.

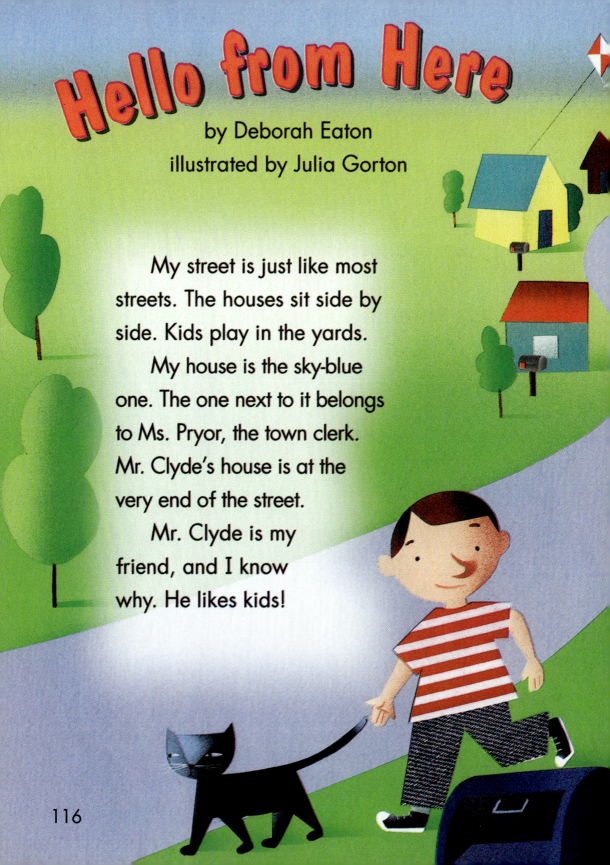

Hello from Here

by Deborah Eaton

illustrated by Julia Gorton

My street is just like most streets. The houses sit side by side. Kids play in the yards.

My house is the sky-blue one. The one next to it belongs to Ms. Pryor, the town clerk. Mr. Clyde's house is at the very end of the street.

Mr. Clyde is my friend, and I know why. He likes kids!

This July, all the kids on the street got a surprise! Mail started to pour into our mailboxes.

July 1
Surprise!
Hi from the sky! My oh my! I've been waiting for years to try sky diving. It feels like flying!
Wish you were here.

117

Who would send us these cards, and why? Who would know our addresses?

July 4
Surprise!
It's so hot in the desert!
My oh my!
I could fry an egg on my saddle.
Look what I found today in a dry creek bed!
I'll sell it and get myself a birthday gift next week.
Wish you were here!

I had to find out who it was. I tried to think like a spy. I looked for clues. Then I realized there were no stamps on the cards! They were not coming on our mail route.

The next morning I hid by our mailbox and waited. Before long a grown person came along, acting sneaky. When he stopped by our mailbox, I jumped up.

"Got you!" I yelled.

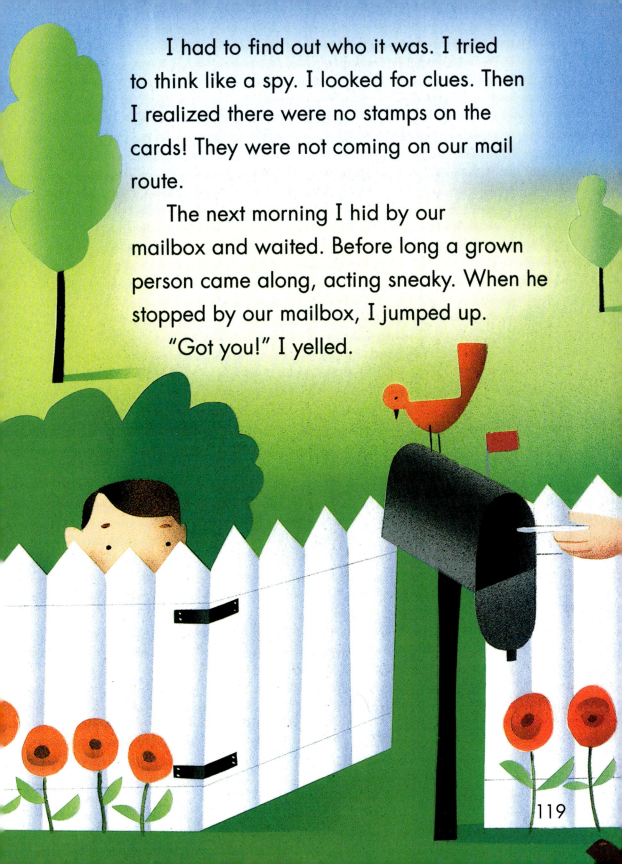

119

"My oh my!" cried Mr. Clyde.
He had a stack of cards in one hand.
He was about to drop one into the mailbox.
"Mr. Clyde!" I exclaimed. "The cards
are fun, but why did you do this?"
"I don't have any grandchildren," he
said. "So all of you are like grandchildren
to me. It was fun to give you cards and
clues. You found out my secret!"

Then it was my turn. I sent cards to all the kids on the street.

You're Invited

July 10
Surprise!
You are invited to a party in honor of Mr. Clyde's birthday. We will play games and fly kites! It will be next Saturday at two. Don't miss the party of all parties!
See you there!

Myles

121

Think About It

1. How does Mr. Clyde feel about the kids on the street? What does he do for them?

2. After talking to Mr. Clyde, how does Myles feel about him? How do you know?

3. After the party, Mr. Clyde will send a postcard to Myles. What will he say? Draw a picture for the postcard, too.

CLICK!

by Celeste Albright illustrated by Michele Noiset

All the kids in our class like Miss Wise. She makes us smile!

"Look at this pin that Kim gave me!" Miss Wise says. "Isn't it a kick?" She has the pin on her hat. It's a fish pin, and the fish has big pink lips.

Mike Briggs says, "Smile, Miss Wise!"

Miss Wise grins.

That's Mike for you. Click, click, click, all the time.

124

"I collect pins," Miss Wise says. "Collecting them is what I do in my leisure time. It can have its disappointments, when I can't get the pin I want. The solution is perseverance!

"See if you like being collectors, kids. Bring a collection to class when you can."

125

Mike visits Tim to see what he's collecting.

"I have nine hats," Tim says. He has on six of them. "Is this a collection?"

"It looks like a collection to me," Mike says.

"Mike, what will you do for a collection?" Tim asks.

"It's not a problem," says Mike. "You'll see. Smile!"

Mike rides off on his bike to see Jill.

"I'm a stamp collector," says Jill. "I like sitting and looking at my stamps."

"That white one with the plane is my favorite," Mike says.

Jill picks it up.

"Smile, Jill!" says Mike.

CLICK!

Then Mike bikes over to Linda's.
"I collect pigs!" says Linda.
"Pigs?" Mike looks uneasy.
"Don't they stink a bit? Do your neighbors get mad? You could compromise with them and collect cats. Cats would be no problem."

Linda chortles. "My pigs are no problem to our neighbors." She invites Mike in to see them.

128

Linda has pigs of all sizes. Many were gifts. She has ticking pigs, big pigs, and five pink pigs.

Linda picks up her favorite, a pig in a hat and wig.

"What do you collect, Mike?" she asks.

Mike grins. He says, "You'll see in class. Smile, Miss Pig in a Wig!"

CLICK!

129

"What's in there, Mike?" the kids ask.

"You are!" Mike says. "Take a look!" There's Tim
in his hats. There are Jill and Linda. All the kids
are there.

"That's quite a collection!" Miss Wise says. "A
smile collection! I like it. Now, you smile, Mike!"

And what a fine smile it is.

Think About It

1. What does Mike collect? How does he collect them?

2. Why do you think Miss Wise asks her class to be collectors?

3. Write a news story about the collections made by the kids in Miss Wise's class.

Joe DiMaggio

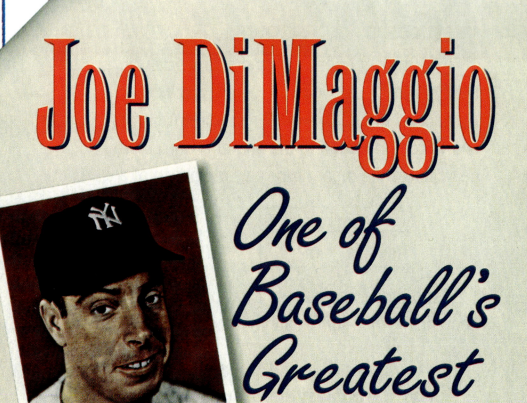

One of Baseball's Greatest

by Tomás Castillo

Joe DiMaggio, the son of immigrant parents, began his baseball career in 1936. He came to the New York Yankees when Lou Gehrig was with them. DiMaggio was 21 and glad to make such a fine team.

The Yankees' manager had hopes for DiMaggio, but Yankees fans were upset. The new man had a bad leg. People asked, "Can he run around the bases? Can he hit in Yankee Stadium?"

In no time, people got to like DiMaggio. They came to the stadium to see him. He was modest, but his hitting was making him a favorite of Yankees fans. Baseball fans from all over agreed that Joe DiMaggio was a tremendous find.

DiMaggio got 206 hits in 1936, and 29 of them were home runs! The Yankees' manager noted that DiMaggio was valuable to the team, and his salary went up.

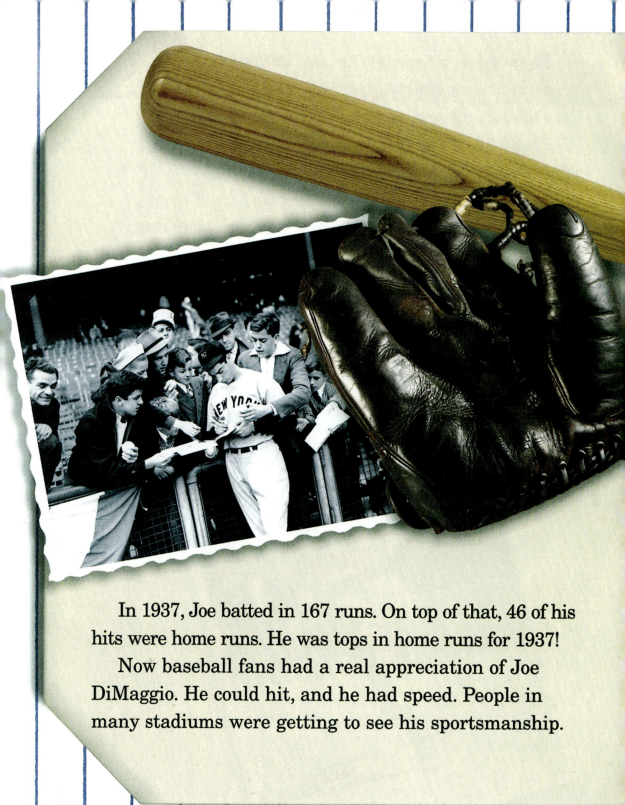

In 1937, Joe batted in 167 runs. On top of that, 46 of his hits were home runs. He was tops in home runs for 1937! Now baseball fans had a real appreciation of Joe DiMaggio. He could hit, and he had speed. People in many stadiums were getting to see his sportsmanship.

DiMaggio still had a "hot bat" in 1938 and 1939. His home runs went down, but his batting went up. In 1939, it was the best in all of baseball.

In 1940, his batting fell off a little. The Yankees slid out of their top spot. The upset manager of the Yankees had to hope his team could be tops again in 1941.

DAILY NEWS

FINAL ★★★★

NEW YORK'S · PICTURE NEWSPAPER

Copyright 1936 by News Syndicate Co. Inc. Reg. U. S. Pat. Off.

Entered as 2nd class matter Post Office, New York, N. Y.

THE LARGEST CIRCULATION IN AMERICA

Vol. 17. No. 268   48 Pages   New York, Monday, May 4, 1936   2 Cents IN CITY LIMITS | 3 CENTS Elsewhere

DIMAGGIO SMACKS 3 HITS IN DEBUT; YANKS WIN, 14-5

—Story on Page 42

The Yankees did win back the top spot, but
Joe DiMaggio outdid his team. On May 15, 1941,
in a game with the Chicago White Sox, he began an
amazing hitting streak. First he got at least one hit in
each of ten games in a row. Then it was 20 games.
When was Joe DiMaggio going to stop getting hits?

For 56 games, DiMaggio got hits. He did not miss one game. On July 17, 1941, in a game with the Cleveland Indians, his hitting streak ended.

Baseball fans will not forget the courageous sportsmanship of Joe DiMaggio. He had a lot of heat on him in 1941, but he met the test. His feat of getting a hit in 56 games still stands.

JOSEPH PAUL DI MAGGIO
NEW YORK A.L. 1936 TO 1951

HIT SAFELY IN 56 CONSECUTIVE GAMES
FOR MAJOR LEAGUE RECORD 1941. HIT 2
HOME-RUNS IN ONE INNING 1936. HIT 3
HOME-RUNS IN ONE GAME (3 TIMES). HOLDS
NUMEROUS BATTING RECORDS. PLAYED IN
10 WORLD SERIES (51 GAMES) AND 11 ALL
STAR GAMES. MOST VALUABLE PLAYER
A.L. 1939, 1941, 1947.

Joe DiMaggio retired from baseball in 1951. The Yankees were sad to see him go. So were baseball fans from New York and all over. In 1955, he was voted into the Baseball Hall of Fame.

DiMaggio had a fine life. He was 84 when it ended on March 8, 1999. He had given a lot to the game he cared about. Baseball fans will not forget Joe DiMaggio. He was one of the greatest.

Think About It

1. Why was Joe DiMaggio voted into the Baseball Hall of Fame?

2. Why did the fans like Joe DiMaggio?

3. Suppose you were in the stands when Joe DiMaggio got a hit in his amazing hitting streak. At home, you wanted to tell about the game in your diary. Write your diary entry.

GARDENS OF THE SEA:
Coral Reefs

by Caren B. Stelson   illustrated by James Noel Smith

If you could look down from space, you would see why Earth is called the blue planet. As the blue parts of a globe show, more than two-thirds of Earth is water.

The world's oceans are teeming with life, with the warmest waters being the richest. Here vast numbers of sea animals make their homes. Here, too, the beautiful coral reefs grow. They are the gardens of the sea.

Coral reefs are found in oceans around the world, but only in the warmest waters. For most corals, the water must be between 75 and 85 degrees—almost like bathwater. It must also be shallow, clean, and clear.

The corals that make up a reef don't grow well below 130 feet. Deeper than that, it's too cold, dark, and still for them. They need sunshine, and they need the flow of the waves to bring their food to them. Each little tube-shaped coral animal has a mouth surrounded by fingerlike sensors. These tentacles catch tiny swimming animals in the gently flowing water.

Coral reefs are found in oceans around the world.

Huge coral reefs like underwater cliffs are made by tiny animals less than $\frac{1}{2}$ inch across. How do they do it?

Each little coral animal attaches itself to the skeletons of those that lived before it. As it grows, it takes calcium from the water and uses it to form a limestone skeleton. When it dies, its hard skeleton remains. Then a new coral animal attaches on top of it. Over time, these very tiny limestone skeletons form a large coral wall. A coral reef grows very slowly—its ridges may be only 3 feet higher in 1,000 years.

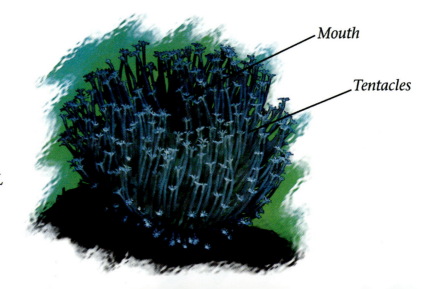

Mouth

Tentacles

CORAL

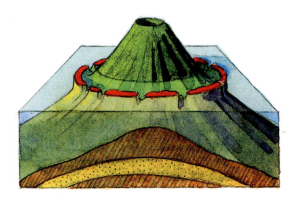

There are three kinds of reefs. A reef may grow around the edge of a volcanic island like fringe around a tablecloth. This is called a **fringing reef**. Most volcanic islands are ancient. Lava no longer flows from their craters.

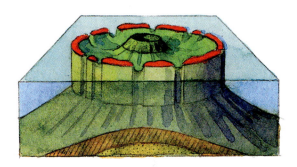

Over the years, the ocean floor may move, and the volcano may begin to sink. Water flows between the volcano and the reef, making a calm lagoon. Now the reef is called a **barrier reef**.

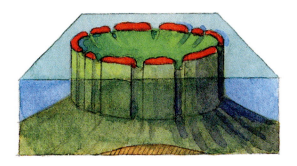

Finally the ancient volcano—crater, lava, and all—disappears. When the island slips under the water, only the reef can be seen. The ring it forms is a **coral atoll**.

143

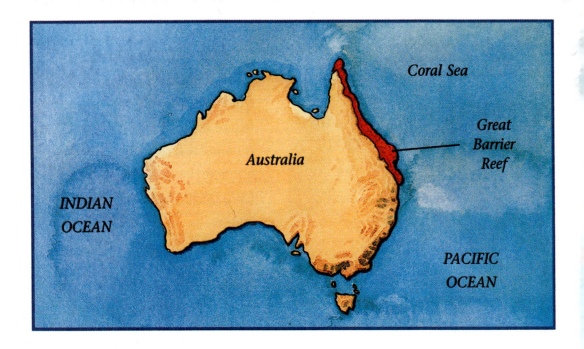

Find the Great Barrier Reef on a map or a globe. Like the Great Wall of China, it is large enough to be seen from space. No other reef is as rich with sea life as this one, the largest on Earth. Rare and colorful sea animals meander in and out of its coral gardens. Scuba divers love to visit this incredible reef to observe and photograph its strange and beautiful sea life. Here are some animals that make their homes in these warm waters.

Sea Horse
Sea horses, like monkeys, have tails that can cling to plants. The males have a pouch in which they carry the eggs until they hatch. The babies use their "monkey tails" to cling together!

144

Longnose Butterfly Fish
These brightly colored fish have long snouts that they use to pluck food from the coral. At night they darken their bodies and sleep in coral caves.

Green Sea Turtle
These huge turtles grow to be 300 pounds and may have 4-foot-long shells. Only the female ever comes ashore. Each year she digs a hole in the sand and lays about 100 eggs.

Giant Clam
The giant clam has the biggest shell on Earth. At almost $\frac{1}{4}$ ton, it is also the largest animal without a backbone.

Crown-of-Thorns Sea Star
This big starfish feeds on coral. There are many more of them lately, so more damage is being done to the reefs.

145

Coral reefs are the gardens of the ocean. Clean, warm, gently moving water and sunlight keep them growing. Without these things, coral life will die, and the reefs will become barren piles of rock. Today, many coral reefs are threatened by pollution. They no longer have the clean water they need to grow in. To save the reefs, we will have to fight pollution. We must care for and preserve our beautiful gardens of the sea.

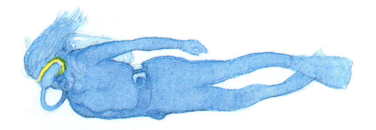

Think About It

1. Where do coral reefs grow?

2. How is a coral reef like a garden? How is it different from a garden?

3. Suppose you've been asked to write a report about one of the animals that live in the warm waters near a reef. Which animal would you choose? Write a paragraph about why you would choose that animal.

147

A MOUNTAIN
BLOWS ITS TOP

A chain of mountains runs along the west coast
of North America. It's called the Cascade Range.
The mountains in this range are beautiful.
Visitors hike and camp there. Loggers cut trees for
lumber. Birds and animals make their homes in
the forests, fields, and rivers.

STORY BY KANA RILEY

These peaks were formed long ago by volcanoes. Deep in the center of our planet is hot melted rock called magma. On top of it float plates of hard rock that form the planet's crust.

In 1980 the plates under the Cascade Range started to shift. The edges of the plates pushed up magma. As the magma rose, it caused the north side of Mount St. Helens to bulge. It made the ground shake. Plumes of steam began to shoot out of the old crater, or hole, at the top. Was the mountain ready to blow? No one knew.

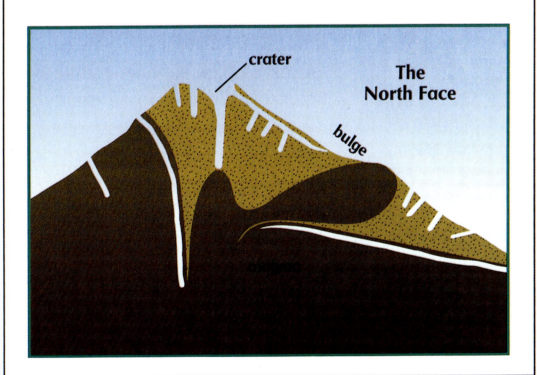

Sunday, May 18, 1980, dawned clear. Snowcapped Mount St. Helens caught the early rays of the sun. All seemed peaceful.

Then suddenly, at 8:32 A.M., the ground began to shake. The epicenter of this quake was very near Mount St. Helens.

This was a big one! With a mighty blast, it cracked the side of the mountain. Magma gushed to the surface, pushing layers of dirt and rocks and water in front of it. Blast after blast rocked the mountain.

Blocks of ice went flying. Water turned to steam. Rocks exploded into dust. Hot ash flew 12 miles into the sky.

Yakima, Washington, is 85 miles from Mount St. Helens. By 9:30 A.M. the sky in Yakima began to grow black. Lightning flashed. It looked as if a storm were coming.

But it was not rain that fell. It was ash. The tiny bits had edges as sharp as glass. They hurt everyone's eyes and made it hard to breathe.

All day ash fell. Soon every surface was covered with layers of it. Workers later swept up more than 600,000 tons from the streets and buildings.

When the big blasts stopped, Mount St. Helens was an awesome sight. The top of the mountain was not there. In its place was a huge, gray hole. From the center of it, clouds of ash still puffed into the air.

The land around the mountain looked like the surface of the moon. All was still. Trees were spilled all over the ground like match sticks. Rivers were choked with mud. Most of the animals had been caught by the blasts. No birds sang.

It has been many years since the mountain blew. What has Mount St. Helens taught us?

It has taught us that our planet is always changing. The blast showed us the awesome damage these changes can cause.

Yet we also saw that in time the land will heal. New plants now grow out of the layers of ash. Animals have come back. The rivers run clear once more.

What's going on inside the mountain? It's not quiet yet. In the center of the crater, another dome of magma is growing. Sometimes steam and ash gush out of it. They help us remember that our planet is still alive and still shaking.

Think About It

1. What happened when Mount St. Helens erupted? What has happened since then?

2. Will Mount St. Helens erupt again? What makes you think as you do?

3. Think about life in Yakima on the day Mount St. Helens blew its top. Write a diary entry as if you were there that day.

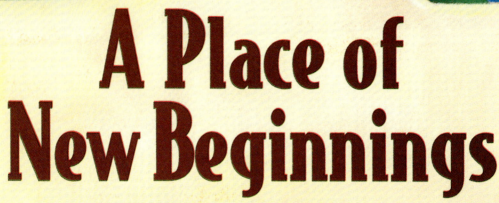

A Place of New Beginnings

by Ben Farrell   illustrated by Jui Ishida

"This is Ellis Island, Karen," Dad said, "where my father's grandfather began his new life. By coming to the United States, Poppa Joe enriched the lives of our entire family."

"Did he come to this place to qualify for citizenship?" I asked.

"No," Dad said. "He came to Ellis Island as a petitioner to enter the United States. Petitioners were obliged to see an examiner here before going to the mainland."

"Why?" I asked.

"That's one of the things we'll learn about on the tour," Dad said.

We started our tour of the Ellis Island Museum in the Baggage Room. People from all over the world once crowded into this hall. They had to leave their baggage here. I could sense the fear that must have gnawed at them, for their baggage was all they had.

Next, we entered the Registry Room. It was a huge hall, with enormous flags hanging above us. Pointing up at them, I asked, "Is this where the people took the oath of allegiance?"

157

"No," Dad said. "They didn't take the oath of allegiance until later, at the citizenship hearing. It takes time and study to become a citizen. This was just the starting place."

"I guess I have a lot to learn," I apologized. "What did happen in this room?"

"This is where the examiner checked passengers' documents," Dad said. "Ships had to provide certificates that gave facts about each passenger."

"What did the examiner check for?" I asked.

"They asked where the person had come from and what he or she intended to do in the United States. Doctors had to check the people, too."

"I guess they had to know if the people were healthy," I said.

"Yes," Dad replied, "but they were mainly checking for diseases. They didn't want to endanger the lives of people living in the United States. Immigrants with a disease were sent back to their homelands."

I looked around the hall. How it must have resounded with noise when it was filled with people! Many would be talking excitedly about getting into the United States. Some would be worrying about being sent back.

"Did Grandpop's grandmother come to Ellis Island, too?" I asked.

"I think so," Dad said, "but no one knows what her name was before she married. The tradition of women changing their names when they marry makes them hard to trace."

"That tradition must be changing," I said. "Some of my friends' moms have kept their names. I think I will, too."

Dad laughed and said, "It's a pity they didn't do things that way in those earlier days." I laughed, too, but I felt a little sad about our family history being lost.

Then Dad said, "Just the same, it might be possible to find out about her. We'd have to do some serious digging."

"Let's do it, Dad," I urged. "I'll help—I like doing research!"

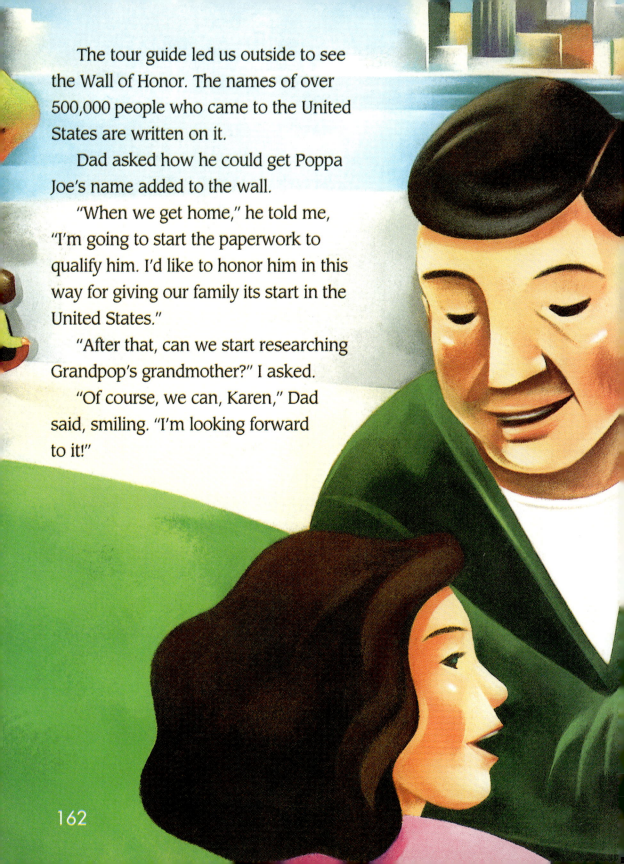

The tour guide led us outside to see the Wall of Honor. The names of over 500,000 people who came to the United States are written on it.

Dad asked how he could get Poppa Joe's name added to the wall.

"When we get home," he told me, "I'm going to start the paperwork to qualify him. I'd like to honor him in this way for giving our family its start in the United States."

"After that, can we start researching Grandpop's grandmother?" I asked.

"Of course, we can, Karen," Dad said, smiling. "I'm looking forward to it!"

Think About It

1. Why do Karen and her dad visit Ellis Island?

2. How do you think Poppa Joe felt when he arrived at Ellis Island?

3. Imagine that you visit Ellis Island and send a postcard to a friend. Write a message for that postcard.

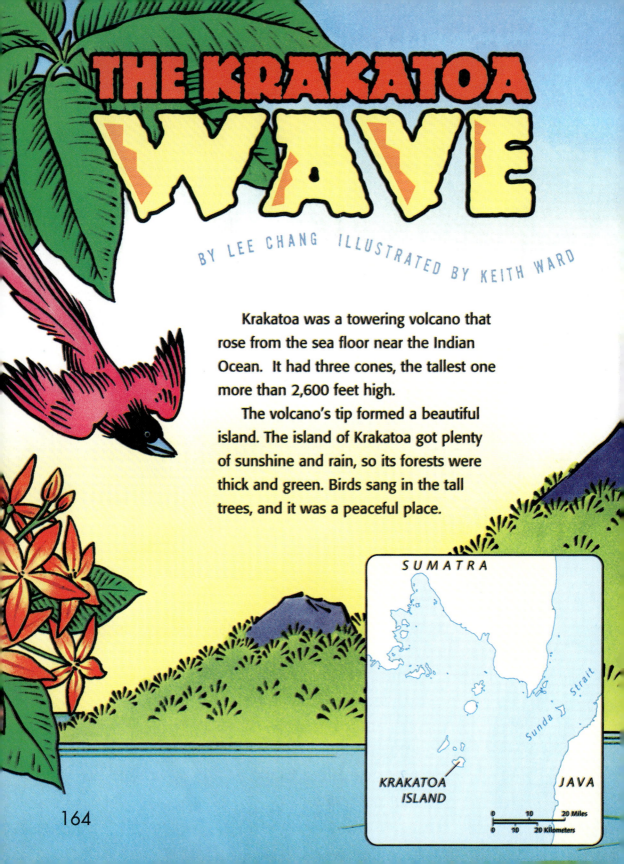

THE KRAKATOA WAVE

BY LEE CHANG   ILLUSTRATED BY KEITH WARD

Krakatoa was a towering volcano that rose from the sea floor near the Indian Ocean. It had three cones, the tallest one more than 2,600 feet high.

The volcano's tip formed a beautiful island. The island of Krakatoa got plenty of sunshine and rain, so its forests were thick and green. Birds sang in the tall trees, and it was a peaceful place.

SUMATRA

Sunda Strait

KRAKATOA ISLAND

JAVA

0   10   20 Miles
0   10   20 Kilometers

In May of 1883, sailors on passing ships saw smoke and ash rising from the top of Krakatoa.

People in Java and Sumatra watched from their coastlines. They saw the smoke, and they could hear small explosions, too. They didn't worry about this. For years, the volcano had just groaned a little and fallen asleep again.

Everything changed on Sunday, August 26, 1883. Krakatoa woke up, this time for good!

A fierce explosion rocked the island, and the ground began to shake with earthquakes. Steam, smoke, and hot ash shot 17 miles into the sky! The ash formed such dark clouds that daytime turned to night.

The ocean began to rise and fall in a crazy way, smashing the boats in the inlet.

Then a gigantic wave rushed from the island to the shores of Sumatra and Java. Earthquakes underwater had generated a tsunami!

The tsunami wasn't like an ordinary high wave. It didn't come from the tidal bulge made by the gravitational pull of the moon. It was powered by the energy of the earthquakes started by the explosion.

The tsunami hit the coastlines hard. Frantic people ran from its path. They rushed to high ground where they might find shelter. They wished the volcano would go back to sleep, but the red glow over Krakatoa got brighter and brighter.

The next morning, great explosions began to pound the air. Krakatoa was blowing apart! The biggest blast could be heard 2,500 miles away. Later, it was said to be the loudest sound ever made on Earth.

Without warning, a new tsunami rushed over the ocean with amazing speed. The wave got bigger and bigger as it crossed the shallow waters near the coastlines. Now it was a monster wave, more than 120 feet high!

The tsunami hit the shores of Java and Sumatra with staggering might. It wiped out 165 towns. More than 36,000 people died. Not a house, not a tree, not a person was left.

The mighty wave went far around the world. It traveled 3,800 miles across the ocean in just 12 hours. (A ship would have taken 12 days!)

More than 100 years have passed, and other tsunamis have come and gone. There will be more in the years to come, but Krakatoa's wave will never be forgotten.

Think About It

1. What is a tsunami? What happened when the Krakatoa tsunami hit Java and Sumatra?

2. Why do you think Krakatoa's wave will not be forgotten?

3. Think about how Krakatoa's island looked before and after the volcano woke up. Write two lists of words and word groups to describe the island. Use your lists to write a paragraph about the island before and after Krakatoa exploded.

The Little Brown Quail

by Cheyenne Cisco

illustrated by Don Sullivan

Brother Quail had a neat little house in the desert, where the wind blew the tumbleweeds. He had dug a swimming hole there, too. All the desert cousins came to his house to lie in the shade. It was good to relax out of the bright sunlight. They sipped tea and ate corn chips. Mmm! Brother Quail made the best corn chips under the sun.

"It's time to make the corn chips!" said
Brother Quail one bright day. "Now, first
things first! Who will help me pick the corn?"

"I will," said Fox, "but wait! I see
something suspicious over by that cactus."
He escaped across the sand.

"I might," said Little Owl, "but I fly
at night. Wake me when there's starlight."
He shut his eyes.

"All right," said Brother Quail. "I will pick the corn myself." And he did. The sun burned bright. The hot desert wind blew. But Brother Quail picked every ear.

"Now, who will help me grind the corn?" he asked.

His quail cousins sighed. "We'd like to," they said, "but not right now. We are off to seek our fortunes." They escaped out the window. Flap! Flap! Flap! They were in flight.

"All right," said Brother Quail. "I will grind the corn myself." And he did. He worked all day and all night.

Brother Quail fried the corn chips, too. When he had asked for help, no one would budge. He might as well have been invisible. Brother Quail gave a sigh. He kept right on working.

In a short time, the kitchen was filled with the delightful smell of fresh corn chips. The smell blew out the window. It tickled the noses of Fox and Owl and all the cousins.

They came running.

"Are the chips ready?" asked Fox.

"Stop right there," said Brother Quail. "Why would I give you any? You did not help me pick the corn. You did not help me grind it. You did not help me fry the chips."

"No," said Owl, "but we'd be glad to help you eat them."

"We'll help next time," said Fox.

Brother Quail sighed. Why fight it? They were his friends and cousins after all. "All right," he said.

All the desert cousins thanked Brother
Quail for the wonderful chips.

"You're welcome," said Brother Quail.
"Now, tell me. Who is going to help clean
up the house?"

"Owl will help you," said Fox.

"Let Fox help you," said Owl.

"Oh, no!" sighed Brother Quail.

Then Fox and Owl laughed.

"We are just kidding," they said.

"We will *all* help you." And they did.

Think About It

1. List three jobs Brother Quail does without help. When do the other animals say they will help him?

2. What suspicious thing do you think Fox sees by the cactus? Why do you think that?

3. Think of a fable or folktale you know well. How would the characters be different if the story took place somewhere else? Choose a new setting for the story, and rewrite it in your words.

A Clever Plan

by María Santos

illustrated by
Sylvie Daigneault

The kingdom of Woodlandia was a good place to live, most of the time. For many years, fine harvests had supplied the people with plenty to eat. Their land was free from famine. Their kingdom was named for its thick woodlands, so the Woodlandians were also plentifully supplied with firewood. The only problem they had from time to time was their king.

King Roger was kind, as a good leader should be. He believed that kindness was very important. He always rewarded his subjects when they were kind to their fellow Woodlandians.

You might ask, "If the king was so kind, what was the problem?" Well, King Roger had a lot of ideas for rewarding his subjects, but his ideas weren't always clever.

One time a kind shoemaker made a pair of wooden shoes for the king. No shoes had ever fit him as perfectly as these did. "If only my subjects were as lucky as I am," he said, sighing. "They would never again have to put up with uncomfortable shoes." Then a not-so-clever idea came to him.

King Roger proclaimed a royal decree. Everyone in every province of the kingdom was to have shoes exactly like his. For, as King Roger knew, the size and shape were perfect.

The same thing happened when King Roger returned with
a pet tiger from a royal journey he took. No pet had ever
pleased him as this one did. He decreed that everyone in
Woodlandia was to keep a pet tiger. For, as King Roger
knew, this kind of pet was perfect.

For a long time the Woodlandians lived with King
Roger's decrees because he was such a kind leader. They did
not want to hurt his feelings, as he would never hurt theirs.

Things changed when the latest royal decree was proclaimed. This is how it happened. King Roger looked at his newest robe, the one with the satin hood. It was trimmed with a thousand gleaming pearls and a thousand glittering emeralds. It sparkled like a billion stars!

Oh, he looked splendid! Who wouldn't feel happy dressed in outfits like his? To bring this joy to his subjects, he decreed that everyone was to dress as he did.

The Woodlandians stood still. They looked at each other. How could they dress like the king? They did not have silks and satins. They did not have billions of pearls and emeralds.

The mayor of Woodlandia understood the problem. He called together the ministers from every province in the kingdom. They looked through rare old books of wisdom, hoping to find a solution.

After many hours, the oldest minister said, "I have an idea."

"Please, tell us what it is!" they implored. When they heard it, all agreed it was a clever plan.

On the day the new dress code took effect, the Woodlandians went to the palace. They wanted to show King Roger their fine robes. The king just stood there, looking confused. Before long, however, he understood what his subjects had done. He shook with laughter until tears trickled down his cheeks.

King Roger took a walk among the people. He looked at each costume with delight. "These emeralds are . . . ?" he asked.

"Grapes, your majesty," the grocer's wife replied.

"Those plumes . . . ?"

"Twigs, your majesty," said the woodcutter.

"People of Woodlandia," announced the king, "I wish to make a royal decree."

"Oh, no!" whispered the mayor, as he shook in his wooden shoes. "Our clever plan didn't work!"

"I proclaim that from now on, before I make a royal decree, I will meet with the ministers of every province. Perhaps they will tell me when my clever ideas are not so clever!"

King Roger was glad that his loyal subjects had shown him his mistake in this kind way. He rewarded them with a royal picnic in the royal woods, and everyone had a royal time!

Think About It

1. What problem do the people of Woodlandia have with their king?

2. What lesson does the king learn about being kind to his subjects?

3. King Roger does not want anyone to miss his royal picnic. Create a poster he could use to announce the event.

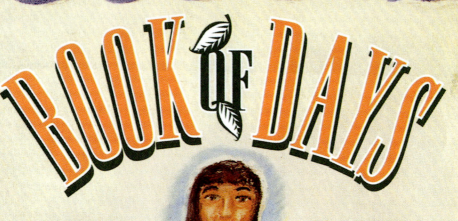

BOOK OF DAYS

written by
Deborah Akers

illustrated by
Mercedes McDonald

Date: April 2

Dear Sue,

I felt so blue after you drove away! Now I have a plan. I will keep each day in this book until my big sister is home again. Then you can read about everything you missed, and I will feel less lonely.

I put myself in charge of your flower box. There were three new green sprouts in the soil. You said there would soon be a rainbow of flowers. I poured a little more water to hurry them along. I could tell they wondered where you were.

Date: April 6

Dear Sue,

Today was a good day. We worked in the garden, and Mom put me in charge of the carrot seeds. I pushed them into the dirt the way you showed me.

Remember last fall, when we dug beds for the plants to sleep in? Most of them are still sleeping, but a few seem to be stirring. The sweet pea sprouts are reaching for the sun with soft, curly fingers.

Date: April 9

Dear Sue,

Today I put myself in charge of the fruit trees. I walked down every row, and counted all the trees that have buds.

Here is a branch from the apple tree. Remember when we picked a basketful of apples? Then you helped me bake my first pie. I felt like a real cook!

The trees seem as if they are holding secrets in their tight buds. I think they are waiting for the right person to share them with. I know just how they feel.

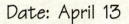

Date: April 13

Dear Sue,

Today was an average day. While Mom went into town, Dad and I walked down to the river. I collected rocks for you on the beach. There were lots of beautiful ones, but I was choosy. I took just a few you could put on your desk.

Guess what happened next? I saw tracks in the sand! Our friend the fox is back, with some baby foxes, too. That must mean spring is really here. When will you be home? You're missing everything!

Date: April 21

Dear Sue,

Today the sky could not stop crying, and your flower box was swimming in rain. I watched from the porch as pools grew in the garden. The fruit trees shook in the storm.

A good thing happened today, too—there was a rainbow. I remembered the special rainbow wish we always make when it rains. I made my wish. Mom said she had a feeling it would come true soon.

Date: April 22

Dear Sue,

Mom was right! I woke up to a sunny day and ran outside. I think the garden must have heard a signal in the night. There were leaves and blooms and little celebrations everywhere!

Then came the best news! You are coming home tonight! Now I am putting myself in charge of the biggest celebration of all!

Think About It

1. Why does the girl write in her book of days? What does she write about?

2. Do you think the girl in the story will go on writing in her book of days? Tell why you think as you do.

3. Imagine that a friend or family member is out of town. Write a journal entry for a special day you would want him or her to know about.